MW01291510

Pumpsie Green and Boston's Struggle to Integrate the Red Sox

MARQUIS PRESS
Chicago, Illinois

Pumpsie Green and Boston's Struggle to Integrate the Red Sox

Robert W. Stone

The research for this essay was conducted while completing a masters program at Harvard University. University and outside resources were utilized.

Stone, Robert W.
Pumpsie Green and Boston's Struggle to Integrate the Red Sox
ISBN 13: **9781530646869**
ISBN 10: **1530646863**

Printed in the United States of America
American History/Sports History/Baseball
African-American History/Race Relations

10 9 8 7 6 5 4 3 2 1

For Elliot and Janie Stone

On August 4, 1959, in Boston,

Massachusetts, a 24-year-old rookie infielder made his Fenway Park debut before 21,034 fans. As he apprehensively stepped from the dugout, bat in hand, he was met with a standing ovation. His arrival had been greatly anticipated for several months and there had been much speculation in the press about increased ticket sales. Some analysts claimed that this young rookie would spark enough curiosity to assure the Red Sox of "more than a million customers for the year.

He was in somewhat of a daze as he glanced out into the crowd. It seemed jam packed; there were people everywhere, even in a roped off section of centerfield that was usually closed. There were more African-American fans in the crowd than had ever been in Fenway before. He knew they were there to see him-- at least half the crowd. Their standing ovation upset his nerves and he tried to stay focused and relaxed. He never liked being in the lead-off spot of the batting order. As he made his way to the plate for the first time, he convinced himself that everything would be all right as long as he didn't strike out. Walking all the way back to the dugout would be too painful; he needed to make contact of some kind.

Trying to control his fears, he stepped up to the plate and looked out to the pitcher's mound. He felt slightly relieved to see Kansas City Athletics pitcher John Tsitouris, a right-hander whom he had faced in the minor leagues; at least he wasn't up against a complete stranger. Taking a deep breath, he got into his left-handed stance, watched the pitcher wind up, and then swung and missed as the first pitch got by him. He tried to relax as the next pitch zoomed passed him with a thud into the catcher's mitt and the umpire called, "ball." His nerves refused to calm and he decided that he would swing if the next pitch came close. The pitch came up and out and over the plate, he swung on it and hit a long line shot that slapped off the left field wall and rebounded behind the left fielder. Still in a daze as the crowd roared, he rounded the bases and slid into third base for a triple.[1] The crowd responded with deafening applause and Elijah "Pumpsie" Green, the first African-American to wear a Red Sox uniform, did his best to compose himself, collect his thoughts and focus on the rest of the game.

The following morning, the *Boston Globe* announced, "Pumpsie Pleases Patrons with Poise!"[2] The *Boston Herald* called him "brilliant," and club manager Bill

Jurges told the press, "Green is the least of my worries. He knows his job on the field and hits for you from both sides of the plate. He acts like he's been around 15 years."[3]

Despite overwhelming praise from fans, the press, and management, Pumpsie Green never felt at home in Boston. "I never relaxed in the major leagues," Green later recalled. "Opening day a lot of guys get the jitters—a little bit of nerves. You're supposed to feel something—a new season starting, all the things that you want to accomplish, all the goals that you set for yourself, and it's the opening day and there you are out there and you want to get off to a good start. I could relax a little bit more on the road, but in Boston I felt like every game was opening day. I never felt comfortable."[4] Pumpsie Green's historical distinction of being the first African-American to play for the Boston Red Sox transcended baseball. Green's presence in Boston was inextricably bound to an immense burden of pressure and discomfort rooted in city and nationwide race relations, the historically strained relationship between the Red Sox and Boston's African-American community, and divergent expectations and concerns projected upon him by the press, the Red Sox and the fans both black and white.

Five years earlier, in 1954, the United States Supreme Court set a precedent that served to hoist race-relations to the forefront of American thought. In the landmark case *Brown v. The Board of Education of Topeka, Kansas*, the Supreme Court unanimously declared "separate but equal" public schools for blacks and whites unconstitutional since segregated black schools were inferior and underfunded. This decision implicitly questioned the entire Jim Crow legal system of the south and segregation in every aspect of American life. Interestingly, the "separate but equal" doctrine had its roots in a precedent that was set by the Massachusetts Supreme Court in 1849, when an African-American man sued the city of Boston for refusing to admit his daughter to a white public school. The case was argued with no success and the Massachusetts Supreme Court rejected the appeal. The "separate but equal" doctrine was further established by the 1896 Supreme Court case of *Plessy v. Ferguson*, and remained intact until the 1954 decision.[5]

Arkansas Governor Orval Faubus' 1957 calling of the state National Guard to block African-American students seeking entrance to Little Rock's Central High School, demonstrated the country's failure to comply with the Supreme Court desegregation order. Although President Eisenhower ordered United States Army troops to escort the nine African-American students to their classes, the incident was indicative of deep racial tensions that rejected government authority. When the federal government did not swiftly enforce its laws and judicial decisions, hopeful and determined African-Americans began to mobilize themselves and demand all of their entitled rights and privileges as United States citizens. By 1959, the civil rights movement, committed to the technique of nonviolent direct action, had overcome many unjust laws through sit-ins, demonstrations, boycotts (most notably the 1955 Montgomery, Alabama bus boycott, initiated by Rosa Parks' refusal to give up her seat to a white man, and fueled by the leadership of Martin Luther King, Jr.), civil disobedience, and the courage to break the law and fill the jails. Despite some encouraging progress, change came slowly and the thrust for racial equality in the United States, particularly in the south, would continuously and tragically face countless incidents of lynching, bombing, drowning, and other terrible acts of violence along its ten-year path toward effective federal legislation.

With its glorified tradition of abolitionist and liberal thinking, Boston, in the midst of a growing civil rights struggle, seemed, at least on the surface, to embody everything that the South was not. But Boston during the late 1950s, like the rest of the country, was faced with its own racial problems—problems hidden within the city's social and political fabric, beneath a facade of northern progressivism. Upon arriving in Boston in the mid-1950s, Doris Bunte, the first African-American woman elected to the Massachusetts state legislature, was initially struck by the city's personable warmth. "It was just amazing to me how friendly people were," Bunte recalls. "People spoke to you at the bus stop, men tipped their hats...but I soon discovered that you could be here for an enormous period of time and they would still be speaking to you at the bus stop, but you wouldn't have any friends and you wouldn't really know anyone...Boston is cold in that regard." For African-Americans specifically, Bunte contends, "[Boston] may be the toughest place in the United States to live. Racism in Boston is deeply rooted and institutionalized."[6]

Systemic racism had a tremendous effect on housing and employment opportunities. As the African-American population of Massachusetts increased 52.9 percent during the 1950s, most minorities found housing in the oldest sections of greater Boston with 60 percent of these citizens living in substandard areas of the city. [7] While a few mixed communities existed in Dorchester and the South End, most African-Americans lived in Roxbury. Widespread segregation stretched throughout the city and into the suburbs through the discriminating practices of property owners, real estate brokers, and bank loan policies. In almost every community where banks had an occasion to finance for non-whites, accommodations were intentionally limited to segregated areas or areas that were becoming segregated.[8]   "We weren't exactly first class citizens," remembers Bunte. "You couldn't go to certain areas if you were black or you'd get beaten up.   You just couldn't go...We were who we were and then there was the rest of the world. We weren't really a part of the mainstream."[9]

With the establishment of the Fair Employment Practice Commission (FEPC) in 1946, Massachusetts made an early effort to prevent discrimination in employment and enforce equal opportunity.   Under the Fair Employment Practice Law, employers with six or more employees, including the state and local governments, were forbidden to discriminate in hiring, discharge, transfer, promotion, and terms and privileges of employment. The commission was empowered to investigate complaints, hold hearings, subpoena witnesses, and obtain Superior Court orders to enforce its decisions.[10] In 1950, the FEPC broadened its scope to include age discrimination, fair education opportunity, public accommodations, and public housing, and changed its name to the Massachusetts Commission Against Discrimination (MCAD).

In 1959, Boston was not ready or willing to live up to the bold expectations set by the MCAD. While the commission continued to receive and investigate complaints, it was largely powerless. The ineffectiveness of this well-intentioned commission may perhaps be best illustrated by Massachusetts' own justice system. According to a 1961 state report on civil rights, Boston's own law enforcement failed to uphold the stipulations of the Fair Employment Practice Law. The report states that "colored members of the police department were not given full opportunity to exercise their talents in police work...most colored officers were put on duty in predominantly colored districts or on cases involving colored people."[11]   In addition to a segregated police department, the report notes that only 3 of 43 probation officers, 1 of a 59-member probation department clerical staff, and 2 of 32 assistant attorneys general were people of color. The report also states that "no clerical personnel of the Negro race were employed in the civil or criminal division of the Superior Court." The excuse given at the time was that "no colored people have applied to the judges for such positions."[12]

The segregation problems that engulfed post-war Boston housing and employment, naturally extended into other facets of society. While the Boston Celtics and Bruins had integrated black players into their organizations by 1959, the Red Sox remained the only professional sports team in the city that had not. The weight of this discrepancy was substantial given baseball's great popularity at the time and its prominent status as our country's national game, a very symbol of democracy. At this time in major league baseball, 12 years after its integration, there were approximately 54 players of color (including seven future hall-of-famers) in the American and National Leagues.[13] Of the 16 major league clubs, and 400 players, the roster of Boston Red Sox team was the only one conspicuously without African-American representation. When confronted with this glaring implication of racism, Red Sox general manager, Stanley "Bucky" Harris stated that no color barrier exists. "Let somebody offer us a Minnie Minoso or a Larry Doby and see how prejudiced we are."[14] With stars like Jackie Robinson, Roy Campanella, Don Newcombe, Willie Mays, Monte Irvin and Hank Thompson leading their team to pennants throughout the 40s and 50s, it was quite obvious to see the disadvantage to excluding African-Americans.[15] Bucky Harris' feeble attempt to attribute the Red Sox failure to integrate to a poor talent pool, is weakened further by the fact that the Red Sox had the first opportunity to sign Jackie Robinson as early as 1945.

Ironically, the last team to field an African-American player could have been the first. In 1944, Boston City Councilman, Isadore H. Y. Muchnick, representing Roxbury, originally a Jewish neighborhood but rapidly becoming predominantly African-American, applied political pressure to the Red Sox. Hoping to insure a big African-American vote in his district, Muchnick threatened to lead a movement to ban Sunday baseball if African-American ballplayers were not given a chance to tryout for the Red Sox. In response to this bold ultimatum, general manager Eddie Collins stated that "the Red Sox would be very happy to have colored ballplayers, but none wanted to play in the big leagues. They were doing better financially in their own leagues"[16] A letter from Wendell Smith, sports editor for the African-American newspaper the Pittsburgh *Courier*, informed Muchnick that Collins' assumption was incorrect. Muchnick let the issue rest, but the following year made the same motion determined to "get tough about it."[17]   Collins quickly responded in a letter to Muchnick, dated March 16, 1945. Reiterating his defense, Collins wrote in part:

> As I wrote...last April, I have been connected with the Red Sox for twelve years and during that time we have never had a single request for a tryout by a colored applicant... It is beyond my understanding how anyone can insinuate or believe that all ballplayers regardless of race, color, or creed have not been treated in the American way so far as having an equal opportunity to play for the Red Sox.[18]

Muchnick seized this as an opportunity to seek such a tryout. After arranging a date with Collins, Muchnick asked Wendell Smith to line up some ball players. Smith, sponsored by the Pittsburgh *Courier*, recruited Sam Jethroe, Marvin Williams, and Jackie Robinson, all stars of Negro League teams. Overconfident, Muchnick prematurely announced that the Red Sox would "open the gates to colored players this year."[19] Muchnick later recalled, "I told Smith to send his men. He did-- and he came with them...On [April 12, 1945] the date we were to have the tryout, President Roosevelt died. Naturally, the date was canceled, and another set...I went to Fenway...and saw Eddie [Collins]... He said, 'you are putting me on the spot, but I'll go through with it.'"[20]   Prior to Muchnick's

Fenway Park meeting with Collins, the three players had been turned away a second and third time on April 14th and 15th. The excuse: no Red Sox scout had seen them play prior to the tryout.[21]

Angered by the delays, Dave Egan, columnist for the Boston *Daily Record* and a thorn in the Red Sox side regarding race relations, blasted Eddie Collins:

> Here are two believe-it-or-not items exclusively for the personal enlightenment of Mr. Edward Trowbridge Collins, general manager of the Boston Red Sox. He is living in anno domini 1945, and not in the dust-covered year 1865. He is residing in the city of Boston, Massachusetts, and not in the city of Mobile, Alabama. To bring him up to the very minute with another item of general knowledge. It is not Abraham Lincoln for whom his flags flutter at half-staff, for he breathed his last on April 15, 1865; it is Franklin Roosevelt for whom the bell tolls, almost 80 years to the day. And both men died for the same high purpose, that other men might be made free.
>
> There! We thought somebody should help Mr. Collins straighten himself out on these little matters...we feel obligated to inform you that since Wednesday last three citizens of the United States have been attempting vainly to get a tryout with his ball team...But Eddie Collins has slammed the door shut and placed his back against it.[22]

The African-American press joined the fray. "There are, throughout the country, " wrote Mabe Kountee of the Boston *Guardian*, "good colored pitchers and catchers of necessary youth and ability to make the Red Sox...The surge is toward democracy in baseball. Nobody is going to stop that surge now. Boston may still be asleep, but we have hopes that she will awaken soon."[23] Boston awakened long enough to hold a tryout for the three players. At 10:30 A.M., April 16, 1945, Robinson, Jethroe, and Williams took the field with a number of young white hopefuls. Aside from an unfortunate and anonymous shouting of "get those niggers off the field," (reportedly by manager Joe Cronin) from somewhere in the stands, the tryout proceeded without incident.[24] Twelve years later, Jackie Robinson recalled the events of the day:

> All of us were in spring training then with our teams...[we] figured it would be a waste of time...There were a dozen or so other players, all white, and all younger than the three of us... When the three of us got our turn to hit, everything stopped... I don't think the Red Sox or any other team had three players put on a demonstration the way we did. Everything fit just right. We were belting the ball off that left-field fence and over it...bouncing balls off that fence like it was handball...We were fielding like we never did before. Jethroe was running faster than he ever did

and catching balls in the outfield he never caught again. We were told they never saw anybody do so well in a tryout and that's the last thing we were told...When the workout was over we were handed application cards to fill out...and we filled them out. Later we all had dinner at a restaurant on Tremont Street and we laughed at them telling us we'd hear from them again.[25]

Red Sox coaches Hugh Duffy and Larry Woodall, who conducted the tryout were certainly impressed with the trio. Manager Joe Cronin was particularly interested in Robinson's speed and commented, "if I had that guy on this club we'd be a world better."[26] Despite this high approval, ten days later, Wendell Smith, not having heard from the Red Sox, wrote to Eddie Collins. Collins wrote back that a broken leg suffered by manager Cronin "threw everything out of gear." Cronin claimed that as manager he had no input in the signing of players, and added that the only openings were in Louisville, and that he didn't think it advisable to send African-Americans there at the time.[27] According to sportswriter Joe Cashman, "Hughie Duffy...told the Red Sox to keep [Robinson]...But Yawkey wanted no part of it. He didn't want to be the one who broke the color line."[28] When the rejection of these players was apparent, the Boston *Chronicle*, fueling anti-

Red Sox sentiments, informed the African-American community that, "Any one of these lads could make the club without a shadow of doubt."[29]

The 1945 baseball season commenced without Robinson, Jethroe, Williams, or any other African American on a major league roster. With disappointment and frustration evoked by the continuing, and seemingly hypocritcal war effort, sportswriter William "Sheep" Jackson of the African-American paper the Boston *Chronicle* lamented:

> Our so-called great national-game is underway, with all teams showing their lily-white personnel. Time and time again interested persons have been trying to find out just why the Big Wigs of the two Big Leagues have ignored the Colored baseball player...Here we are in the biggest war of all time with the American white and colored soldiers fighting side by side...while here in the states...people are still upholding to the principles of racial discrimination, the very thing against which we are fighting Germany—to rid the world of such practices...Let's get our own house in order before we try to save the world. Our world is right here...This isn't the national game and will never be until the colored American is given the opportunity to play in the Big Leagues.[30]

Along with disappointment and frustration came the hope of grass-roots inspired change. At the start of the 1945 season, an editorial in the Boston *Chronicle* read: "Our chance is coming some day in the not too far distant future, there is no mistake about that. Moreover, there will be nothing the owners can do about it... the public is going to start asking questions, and the Colored folks themselves are going to get mad and start howling. The time is ripe now, but we must do it their way through their system."[31]

No African-American would be signed by any major league team until the following year when Branch Rickey and the Brooklyn Dodgers organization recruited and signed Jackie Robinson, sparking the eventual integration of the other 15 teams. Ironically, the Boston African-American press, in 1945, dismissed Brooklyn's simultaneous tryout for African-American ball players speculating that the Boston try-out was "more significant than those held with the Brooklyn Dodgers."[32] In Boston, integration notwithstanding, tensions continued to mount for the next 14 years as African-Americans, hoping to see a black face on their home team, sought to understand the Red Sox's relationship with the city and attempted to work "through their system."

The "system" or "relationship" between Boston sports and state and local politics is undeniable. The Boston Red Sox organization has always been important to city and state politics. "Most politicians are men, and most men like sports," says Doris Bunte. "The teams [in Boston] are important enough to get the politicians to shape business...I have seen, as State Representative, an informal day in the House of Representatives because people were going to the [Red Sox] opening game."[33]   Aside from its recreational role in the personal lives of local politicians, the Red Sox baseball club holds a prominent and influential spot in Boston society. Based on her experience in Boston politics, Bunte rated the socio-economic importance of the Red Sox to Boston a nine on a scale from one to ten.[34] The wide popularity of the Red Sox, through both winning and losing seasons, indicates a public interest too strong to be overlooked in the shrewd maneuvering of Boston politics. Hence, governors and mayors concerned with their public image continue to declare "Red Sox days" and eagerly volunteer to throw out the first pitch on opening day. The Red Sox, similarly, depend upon Boston's political system for operating permits, public transportation, parking, and a host of other components that assure the smooth operation of the club. Since the relationship between Boston and the Red Sox is mutually beneficial, a friendly, working relationship is in the best interest of both the city and the team's management. In 1959, neither the Red Sox, nor the city of Boston were prepared to face the ramifications of political and social changes that would threaten to jeopardize this relationship. The practical issue of parking seemed pressing enough.

"By 1960 nearly 80 percent of American families had at least one car, and 15 percent had two or more. There were more then 73.8 million cars registered, as opposed to 39.3 million ten years earlier."[35] To baseball, increased automobile sales, along with growing suburban towns and a baby boom that caused America's population to jump a staggering 29 million within the decade, meant more fans to fill the stands if the ball parks could become automobile friendly. The Red Sox, seeking to capitalize on this situation, raised the issue of insufficient parking with the city of Boston and Mayor John B. Hynes. Not surprisingly, the Red Sox had placed the mayor under great political pressure to assist them with their problem. "I would assume," stated business manager Dick O'Connell, "that Mayor Hynes and his committee have come up with some plan. I sure hope they have as we need more space for our customers. We cannot afford to drive them away by not furnishing them adequate facilities."[36] While nothing happened in 1958, Hynes promised that something official would be done in 1959. One proposal to build a 4,000 car facility on land that had been used as a World War II vegetable garden and was property of Boston's Park Department, was discussed. The parking spaces would benefit both Boston and the Red Sox, providing patrons a place to park for the game, and earning the city an estimated $250,000 yearly income. Another proposal pushing for a 1,200 car lot on the same property, would cost the city an estimated $189,000. Both proposals met stiff opposition from "Victory" gardeners.[37] The Red Sox garnered public support and simultaneously avoided financial responsibility for the construction project by stating, "[we] don't want anything out of the parking lot except the convenience of having it for our fans."[38]

In the wake of the Dodgers' and Giants' move to California, Hynes would do anything he could to avoid "a city of fans who believe that the mayor ran the team out."[39] The Red Sox only contributed to this pressure by denying certain rumors while inciting other fears. "General Manager Bucky Harris," *The Sporting News* reported, "heatedly denied that Owner Tom Yawkey might move the Red Sox out of Boston because of the parking situation. 'But he might get so mad about the thing that he'd sell the club...'" And just in case the now frantic Red Sox fans missed the point, Harris added "'...and that wouldn't be good. Mr. Yawkey is the greatest owner in the game, baseball couldn't afford to lose him.'"

Tom Yawkey, at age 30, purchased the struggling Red Sox franchise from Bob Quinn in 1933, for one million dollars. Passionate about baseball and sport in general, Yawkey hired Eddie Collins as his first general manager in an effort to lead the Red Sox to a winning season. Throughout his years as Red Sox owner (until his death in 1976), Yawkey would continuously spend millions in efforts to purchase players that he thought would help the club grasp a pennant. His passion for baseball was so genuine that he rarely missed a home game. A private, reserved man, very little is known about Yawkey's personal life or moral convictions. There is a wide range of speculation about his character, however. Yawkey has been remembered as everything from a controlling racist to a laid-back man-of-the-people. While there is absolutely no consensus on this issue, it is generally accepted that Yawkey valued loyalty tremendously, felt contempt for the press, had great political influence in Boston, and protected his privacy. Even in his public role as Red Sox owner, Yawkey rarely made appearances. In 1959, however, with the Red Sox fielding one of its worst teams in history, and suspiciously remaining the only major league team without an African-American player, eyes turned questioningly to the owner's box.

A brief statement made by Jackie Robinson, while visiting Boston in January, 1959, started a ball rolling that would ultimately force both the Red Sox and Bostonians to confront race-relations and re-examine the social and political foundations of the city. "Jackie Robinson Rips Red Sox Prejudices," claimed the January 31, headline in the *Chicago Defender*.

Jackie Robinson, major league baseball's first Negro player, charged the Boston Red Sox were "prejudiced" against his race. "You can quote me on this: They are prejudiced." the ex-Brooklyn Dodger first baseman said. Robinson...said Red Sox management and not Boston fans were guilty of the prejudice...Tom Yawkey has owned the Red Sox for a long time and has missed a couple of pennants by a game or two. "Maybe if he had a good Negro player on the team he might have won those pennants," Robinson said.[40]

The Red Sox were not prepared to confront an accusation this powerful from a public figure with Robinson's national stature. Since the Detroit Tigers had called Ozzie Virgil up to the majors in 1958, the Red Sox were alone. The country watched and anticipated their response.

One month later, to great surprise, the Red Sox did not respond with their traditional excuse that they couldn't find any good African-American players. Instead, they reached into their Minneapolis farm team, and announced that minor league infielder, Elijah "Pumpsie" Green would join the Red Sox for spring training in Scottsdale, Arizona. While Green had played well in Minneapolis under the management of Gene Mauch, calling him up to spring training seemed premature. The decision may have been an impulsive response to Robinson's criticism and an attempt to refute accusations of racism for the last time. In any case, the ensuing circumstances indicated that the Red Sox organization had failed to prepare for or anticipate potential racial issues.

As Pumpsie Green arrived in Scottsdale, the press celebrated his arrival. "Boston Red Sox Hailing First Negro Ball Player!" exclaimed the Chicago *Defender*. [41] "Pumpsie hit .356 in Panama during the winter season and should report in at top condition," wrote *The Sporting News*.[42] Pumpsie's arrival was "a shot in the arm for baseball in

Boston...What we want to see...is Pumpsie actually playing at Fenway Park...colored people are still skeptical..." an African-American leader said.[43] This hopeful skepticism initially dissipated as reports of Green's spring training performance reached Boston. The Boston *Daily Record* proclaimed, "Pumpsie Came to Play and Stay."[44] "Pumpsie Swinging Sizzling Stick," hailed The *Sporting News* and reported, "Elijah "Pumpsie" Green is making quite an impression in the Red Sox camp...and show[s] no sign of cooling off...he's hit and hit hard...To say that Pumpsie is the outstanding rookie in the camp would not be challenged."[45] After the first 11 games and 36 at bats, Pumpsie had hit 3 home runs, 16 hits, 8 runs batted in, and held a batting average of .444.

While Pumpsie Green's spring training performance was exceptional on the field, his very presence on the squad soon gave rise to a slew of racial issues. Although he was well aware of his distinction as the first African-American on the Sox, Green wanted only to play baseball. He did not wish to be a center of controversy, nor did he desire the responsibility of fighting for civil rights in baseball. He only wanted to play the game. This proved to be impossible since everywhere the team played, players and fans constantly reminded Green of his unique position. Many African-American players, with strong opinions regarding Tom Yawkey and the Red Sox, shared their ill-feelings with Pumpsie. From the stands, some racist whites, upon seeing Green in the field, took the opportunity to voice their hatred: "Hey Pumpsie, you think you'll ever get to Boston?...Hey Pumpsie, you'll never play with Ted Williams, you're not white enough...Hey Pumpsie, why do you think you can play in Boston?...no other niggers have ever played in Boston."[46] Off the field, Green, did not stay in the same hotel as the rest of the team. In fact, Green didn't even stay in the same city. *The Sporting News* covered the story under the headline, "First Negro With Red Sox Assigned Commuter's Role":

Pumpsie Green...is not staying at the club's fashionable hotel headquarters [in Scottsdale, Arizona], but officials denied that segregation restrictions were responsible. Jack Malaney, publicity director of the Red Sox, insisted that accommodations for the rookie were not available at the swanky hotel because of the seasonal tourist rush. Several other Red Sox players are not registered at the hotel, but have been assigned to other Scottsdale hostelries.[47]

The claim that Green was not registered in the team's hotel because there was no room is flimsy. Even if the Red Sox did have a limited number of rooms, one would think that Green would be given one if only to avoid a scandal. Instead, the Red Sox put him up, alone, in a very nice hotel 20 miles away in Phoenix. Green was provided a driver to take him back and forth from Scottsdale Stadium to the Frontier Motel in Phoenix. As an African-American, Green was welcome nowhere in Scottsdale. Apparently, segregation wasn't significant enough to stop Scottsdale's Camelback Inn from stating in their ads that "the entire Boston organization has made a hit with everyone here," or Scottsdale's tourism department from advertising, "Scottsdale, Arizona... The West's Most Western Town...Welcomes the Boston Red Sox!"[48]   The next season, after much criticism, the Red Sox made arrangements for Green to stay in Scottsdale. This was still unsatisfactory, however, since Green again stayed in a hotel separate from the rest of the team and because deep segregation in Scottsdale prevented Green from having any kind a social life. Ironically, if Pumpsie wanted to socialize, he was forced to hire a car to take him to Phoenix, where the San Francisco Giants were stationed. At the Adams

Hotel, the Giants' players, black and white, stayed together.

Insensitive to Green's segregated conditions and unaware of his own prejudice, sportswriter John Gillooly of the Boston *Daily Record* wrote that Pumpsie "was treated just about as fine as one of his complexion could be treated in that prejudiced portion of our geography."[49]

The African-American press did not treat the issue as lightly. "Green is walking a lonely road," wrote Abe Attucks in the Boston *Chronicle* , "Unable to stay with his own team...He ate alone, went to shows alone, and only became a part of the team on the playing field. This might have been excusable in 1945. It certainly cannot be justified in 1959."[50]   Green's assertion that he only wanted to make the grade as a major leaguer, was not enough for Boston's African-American community.   Attucks' implication that the African-American community expected more from Green than simply playing the game on the field is articulated further in his column. "It is more important that Green becomes an American before he becomes a Red Soxer," wrote Attucks. "Bay State fans...will be rooting for [Green] to not only make the team, but to be accepted in full equality."[51]   Pumpsie Green's plea that he did not want to become a "controversial stormcenter" was ignored. He had already become a symbol of hope for the African-American community.

In the white press, Pumpsie Green's spring training was, on the surface, far less symbolic. Boston sportswriters for the *Herald*, *Globe*, and *Daily Record* focused primarily on Green's statistics, which position he would be playing, and whom he might replace on the field. Several reporters paid particularly close attention to the struggle between the young rookie and veteran shortstop Don Buddin, speculating that Green might take over the position if Buddin didn't improve. The subtext, to these articles, was that the young, African-American newcomer would take away the job of an experienced white player. "Praise for Enemy: Buddin Fears Green," appeared as a headline in the Boston *Daily Record*. The article itself is scattered with references to Green as an enemy, outsider, and threat to current players' job security. After praising Green's abilities, columnist John Gillooly noted, "there is...one notable exception to this evaluation of Green...Don Buddin. It is his job that Green is after. 'He looks real good. He's got me worried,' says Buddin in praise of the enemy with whom he is friendly. Not friendly enough, of course, to go fishing.

But cordial."[52]   Later in the column, Gillooly again raises the issue of Green stealing jobs: "Pumpsie is going along noiselessly but impressively in his campaign to be the first colored boy to play with the Red Sox," he begins with a trace of condescension, "He may not have the equipment to win the shortstop job...but he's going to put out one of the reserve infielders... they're worried...they too are disturbed by Green's versatility."[53] In this instance, Green is both condemned and praised for his ability. If he played well, he was the "enemy," if he performed poorly he didn't belong in the club-- he was being set up to fail.

Throughout the 1959 spring training, there had been much speculation about whether or not the Red Sox would actually field an African-American player during the regular season. Some felt, that despite Green's success, he was young, inexperienced, and might be better served to play another season with a Triple A club. For others, the significance of Pumpsie's promotion to the Red Sox transcended his ability. By the end of spring training, Green had led the team in both batting average and home-runs, and was voted the Red Sox top rated rookie by 11 Boston sportswriters. His ascent to the Red Sox seemed certain. Just two days before the start of the 1959 season,

John Gillooly wrote, "Those who said... 'Pumpsie' Green would not be carried into the regular season must eat their words. Green...will be on the bench in Yankee Stadium when the race starts Friday."[54] In Houston, later that day, Red Sox manager Mike "Pinky" Higgins pulled Pumpsie aside and with absolutely no explanation ordered, "get all your baggage...you're going to meet the Minneapolis Millers." "You got it," Green replied in no position to question the decision.[55] He was the only casualty on the eve of the opening game.

The farming of Pumpsie Green made national headlines: "Sox Send Green to Minneapolis Farm: Field Brass Decides Pumpsie Has No Chance to Displace Buddin;"[56] "Red Sox Prevent Precedent;"[57] "Timing Bad in Dropping Green!"[58] "Pumpsie Brush off Puts Sox on Spot."[59] The response from the press was immediate and varied. "Even the usually disinterested whites are rebellious. There's disturbing talk of boycotts, pickets in the troubled air," wrote the Boston *Daily Record*.[60] "It is hoped that the incident will be permitted to remain what it is...a routine case of a rookie's being sent down for more seasoning," said the Boston *Herald*.[61] John Gillooly's column was more concerned with Don Buddin, "Pruning of Pumpsie Could

Hurt Buddin."[62] Gillooly worried that fans would take out their disappointment on Buddin in the form of loud boos and hisses.

Most fans blasted the Red Sox. "It's darn foolish,"[63] said one fan, "According to the write up I think he's a better all-around player than Buddin."[64] "I think he should be given a better chance to make the grade," stated a fan from Revere.[65] "There's too much prejudice on the part of Yawkey," claimed a East Boston resident.[66] "Yawkey doesn't like colored players anyhow, that's pretty obvious," said a fan from Somerville.[67]

Ted Williams stated that "Green...would be better off playing in the minors every day than sitting on the bench with the Red Sox."[68] Manager Mike Higgins, who had once been quoted as saying, "There'll be no niggers on this ball club as long as I have anything to say about it,"[69] announced to the press, "We just decided he's not yet a major leaguer, and that's all there is to it."[70] Pumpsie Green, though he wasn't happy about the decision, refused to comment. In those days, with the Reserve Clause still in effect, there was "no free agency. They could put you in the minor leagues and throw away the key."[71]

While most of the white press in Boston saw the demotion as a poor public relations, but a reasonable baseball decision, the black press viewed the incident as an act against Pumpsie's citizenship. Sending Green down, symbolically deprived Boston's African-American community of democratic opportunity. It also served to further ostracize African-Americans and reinforce the feeling that black and white worlds were separate in Boston. The incident naturally caught the attention of Herbert E. Tucker, president of the Boston branch of the NAACP. Tucker, a courageous, well-educated African-American community leader, felt a personal obligation to bring pressing but sensitive issues into the public eye. Representing the NAACP, he forwarded an angry telegram to members of the Boston City Council, the Massachusetts senators, and the Massachusetts Speaker of the House of Representatives. It said:

> We call upon you and your honorable body to vote against the granting of the use or conveyance of any public land to the Boston Red Sox baseball organization. We feel very strongly that any business that would sacrifice the principles of fair play and the American way of life-- as was evidenced in the treatment accorded Pumpsie Green during the spring training of the Red Sox and the subsequent results thereof-- should not be

allowed to financially benefit by utilizing public lands for their private use.

Although there have been claims to the contrary--the evidence over the years leads us to believe that the Boston Red Sox condone racial segregation and discrimination and thereby create an atmosphere that makes it all but impossible for the most qualified to succeed.[72]

In reaction to the telegram, the Boston *Chronicle* wrote that the Boston African-American "community sentiment is for once wholly in accord...Indignation is as hot as molten steel brimful in a cauldron. It will cool even while the unity of freedom-loving Bostonians forges swords which will defeat the oppressive dragons of Jim Crowism on and off the diamond."[73]

On April 11, soon after sending the telegram, the NAACP, along with the Boston Ministerial Alliance, filed a formal request with the Massachusetts Commission Against Discrimination to investigate the "unfair and undemocratic" employment policy of the Red Sox. Herbert E. Tucker told the press, "I am in no way trying to abrogate their authority to determine the value of a player. Green is just one facet since 1947. I am asking the commission to instigate an investigation into their entire hiring policy—

athletes, ticket sellers, grounds-keepers. Green was just the straw that broke the camel's back. It's part of their entire pattern."[74] The MCAD took the complaint under advisement and agreed to investigate the Red Sox for possible violation of the Fair Employment Practices Act. "We will probably look into the entire hiring policy at Fenway Park, which would include everyone, not just players, " said Walter Nolan, executive secretary of the committee.[75] As the commission promised to investigate the charges, a Tufts student picketed Fenway Park. His signs read: "Race hate is killing baseball in Boston," and "We want a pennant not a white team."[76]

While the NAACP voiced their concerns and the MCAD conducted their investigation, Tom Yawkey and the Red Sox were playing the game of politics. The day following the MCAD's agreement to investigate the Red Sox, Yawkey granted rare interviews to certain members of the Boston press. The topic was not the Pumpsie Green affair, but rather the future of the Red Sox. "Will Yawkey Quit Boston?" read a Boston*Globe* headline.[77] Jerry Nason wrote, " that the Pumpsie Green story has developed dangerously...is the understatement of the year. The greatest danger in it is that Tom Yawkey, one of the top owners, might be agitated to the point of quitting baseball...and the Red Sox...Yawkey is the sort of man who gets his back up when he feels anybody is trying to interfere with his operations." Nason then recalled a conversation when Yawkey asked him, "'What do you think would happen if the Red Sox ever left Boston?'... [Nason] replied, 'As a sports town it would probably break Boston's back.' 'Exactly' said Yawkey snapping his fingers, 'and I could do it like that...not that it's probable, but it's possible. They are cutting my throat and I don't like it. Nobody had better call it a bluff. I don't bluff.'" After describing this conversation, Nason offered some final thoughts: "This is a guy I would not push too hard. He's taken a lot of knocks without a whimper and he's been a tremendous asset to this town. I'd find the rights and wrongs of the Pumpsie Green situation, but I'd tread very carefully while doing so."[78]

In addition to planting threats with the press, Yawkey was certainly communicating with city politicians. He found an ally in Mayor John Hynes who dutifully declared April 14th, as "Red Sox Day" in Boston. Hynes publicly praised the Red Sox, pointed out their value to the city, and stated, "Boston would be a minor league city without the Red Sox...We want to keep the Red Sox and that's why Boston wants to give part of its park land to the Sox, that's the least we can do."[79]   Hynes seemed unconcerned with both the ongoing investigation and the NAACP's request to prevent the parking garage project-- essentially dismissing the concerns of the whole African-American community of Boston. Racial problems apparently didn't weigh too heavily into Hynes' agenda. "Red Sox Day" notwithstanding, the MCAD investigation, public outcry from both black and white citizens, and the parking issue surely created considerable tension between the Red Sox and city politicians.   It was becoming increasingly more compromising for the city to uphold its end of the reciprocal relationship.   Ultimately, the Red Sox would not get their parking garage. Instead, a public transportation line was built stretching from the western suburbs to the city with a Fenway stop along the way.

"I deny categorically that the Red Sox have a discriminatory policy...The Boston Red Sox are entirely American... We think these charges have been unfair," stated Red Sox business manager Richard O'Connell in an attempt to defend his team.[80]   Next, O'Connell issued a statement indicating that the Red Sox did not reject Jackie Robinson in 1945. After the tryout, O'Connell told the

MCAD, "Robinson was told he could be signed to a contract with one of our clubs... He was told he could go with Louisville or Rocky Mount and possibly Scranton... Obviously he didn't sign with us."[81] As for general hiring policies, O'Connell stated that "few Negroes applied for any type of job...in the past several years, four had been hired in the concessions at Fenway Park. Of these, two died, one has been dismissed after three weeks employment."[82] In addition to defending the team's policies, O'Connell expressed his distaste for the MCAD's interference: "We have a right to manage our own ball club...People from City Hall and the State House don't hire people for us. We hire them."[83] This obvious resentment of government involvement further indicates the strain in the Red Sox relationship with the city.

The discrimination investigation continued to draw public attention. Abe Attucks of the Boston *Chronicle* editorialized:

> The regime of Yawkey has, in effect, broken some important laws, one of them trampled the rights of a 24 year old youth who is being"brain washed" to say he is happy behind the Sox Iron Curtain...Green may or may not finally end up in Boston...the Red Sox do not have to depend on [Pumpsie Green]. They can acquire other sepia stars through sale or trade. But Yawkey has yet to

> prove he really wants a colored player. Whether he
> does or not, the people of Boston do.[84]

While sentiments of this sort flooded African-American newspapers, white papers primarily focused on the regular events of the baseball season, until the Red Sox organization responded to the MCAD. Throughout the investigation, Pumpsie Green refrained from speaking before the commission.

The MCAD consisted of Mildred H. Mahony, Walter Nolan, Emanuel Goldberg, and Walter C. Carrington, all well-intentioned people involved in trying to improve the state. Realistically, there was not much that the commission could do in terms of the Red Sox-Pumpsie Green case. While the commission invited both Yawkey and Harris to represent the Red Sox position, neither accepted, keeping the investigation at a standstill. Most of the MCAD's previous investigations had been concluded, not through subpoenas or court orders, but rather through conciliation. This case was clearly becoming too big for an organization that couldn't even regulate the justice system with which it was affiliated. It is not outlandish to speculate that the solution to this delicate matter may have been predetermined, and the investigation simply obligatory procedure. While little is known about the closed-door conversations of this commission, Doris Bunte, nearly 40 years later, suggested a hypothetical, yet realistic account:

> The NAACP files charges and makes accusations...the MCAD has a little group that is going to go in and investigate...The group gets told by the Governor, who appoints them to the commission, that it's not good for the city...This happens all the time...They were right to have raised it, you're right to investigate it, but it is not good for the city...What we are going to need to do is... decide that [the Red Sox] should be more inclusive...but not go after them, not have any real findings, not have anything negative...We don't want to start something in Boston with the summer coming...we don't want this to get out of control.[85]

Regardless of whether or not this scenario ever took place, the Commission unanimously accepted the first response from the Red Sox-- a written guarantee by general manager Stanley "Bucky" Harris. The guarantee was accepted as an "evidence of good faith," and the Red Sox were easily cleared of all charges. The guarantee stated:

> There will be no color barrier in the operations of the team...players will be scouted and hired without regard to color. Suitable non- segregated accommodations will be available for all members of the Red Sox during future spring training sessions. The Red Sox offer an equal opportunity to all to apply for employment, and all applicants will be considered on a non-discriminatory basis.[86]

Since these expectations were accepted only as evidence of good faith, the Red Sox were under no legal responsibility to ensure their follow through. The end of the investigation was signaled by the optimistic headline in the Boston *Chronicle*, "Red Sox Pledges End of Discrimination." Hope was restored.

Slightly over a month after the conclusion of the investigation, after firing manager Mike "Pinky" Higgins and replacing him with Bill Jurges, Pumpsie Green was called up to the Red Sox. Every major league team was now integrated. The fanfare resumed with the same exuberance it had shown during spring training. "Green Ends What Robinson Started,"[87] "Pumpsie First Negro to Make Sox,"[88] "Pumpsie Green: Man with a Mission,"[89] "Here's Hoping Pumpsie Makes It This Time,"[90] "Pumpsie Pierces Red Sox Iron Curtain."[91] Sadly, though, just prior to Green's promotion even some of his former supporters had abandoned him. African-American columnist Abe Attucks wrote, "Pumpsie Green actually has lost a lot of favor with colored fans...after the Red Sox stated Green himself would keep out of the case...Green is a young man but he has got to live with his people and share our hurts all his life...He should never oppose the NAACP or any organization that seeks to make his role lighter. A job with the Red Sox is not worth it!"[92] While the African-American press criticized Green's silence, the white press showed its approval. "...He did not take the opportunity to talk about ill treatment...A smart boy. There is nothing to be gained by creating a furore..." wrote Bob Holbrook of the Boston *Globe*.[93]

Pumpsie Green had made it to the Boston Red Sox. Unfortunately, however, the cost was great. Months of controversy had taken their toll on the young ball player. The city of Boston had been forced to confront difficult issues of racism and equality. Boston's very foundations of social and political life had to be reassessed; sports, politics, communities, race-relations, and countless other assumptions had been disrupted. For many, Pumpsie Green symbolically stood as a reminder of all that had been called into question. His presence meant different things to different people and the myriad of expectations placed upon him left an indelible mark on his psyche. There was no way to please everybody; simply being a ballplayer wasn't enough. Chicago *Defender* sportswriter Lee D. Jenkins poignantly described the conflicting pressures that Green would face every time he stepped up to the plate:

If he boots one out it'll be 'I told you so' from one
segment of the populace. If he he handles major
league pitching it'll be 'we knew it all the time from
another segment. Pumpsie is in the middle and it's
going to take more than the work of his bat and
glove...his ability to handle the pressures over and
above his baseball skills will bring the final answer
to the Pumpsie Green case.[94]

Despite increased ticket sales and great anticipation, these
tensions would prove to be too much for Pumpsie Green.
Even though he launched a triple in his first at bat in Fenway
Park, the pressure would ultimately prevent him from ever
relaxing and just playing the game of baseball-- something
that most other ballplayers simply took for granted.

*Elijah "Pumpsie" Green played Major League Baseball for 5
years finishing with 796 at bats and a lifetime batting average
of .246. In 1963, the Red Sox traded him to the New York
Mets where he spent the remainder of his Major League career.*

NOTES

---

[1]. This entire introduction is based on: interview with Pumpsie Green; Boston *Globe* , August 5, 1959; and Boston *Herald*, August 5, 1959.

[2]. Boston *Globe* , August 5, 1959.

[3]. Boston *Herald*, August 5, 1959.

[4]. Interview with Pumpsie Green.

[5]. Kirshon, John W., Chronicle of America (New York: Simon and Schuster, Inc., 1989) 766.

[6]. Interview with Doris Bunte

[7]. *Report of the United States Commission on Civil Rights*, 1959, 1961.

[8]. *Report of the United States Commission on Civil Rights*, 1959.

[9]. Interview with Doris Bunte

[10]. Massachusetts Commission Against Discrimination, *Civil Rights Statutes Administered by the Massachusetts Commission Against Discrimination*, 1959.

[11]. *Report to the United States Commission on Civil Rights from the State Advisory Committee*, 1961.

[12]. *Report to the United States Commission on Civil Rights from the State Advisory Committee*, 1961.

[13]. Michigan *Chronicle*, April 25, 1959.

[14]. Chicago *Defender*, March 7, 1959.

[15]. Golenbock, Peter; Fenway; An Unexpurgated History of the Boston Red Sox (New York: G.P. Putnam's Sons, 1992) 221.

[16]. Boston *Globe*, April 29, 1959.

[17]. Interview with Isadore H. Y. Muchnick, Boston *Globe*, April 29, 1959.

[18]. Boston *Daily Record*, April 16, 1945.

[19]. Boston *Guardian*, April 14, 1945.

20. Interview with Isadore H. Y. Muchnick, Boston *Globe*, April 29, 1959.

21. Golenbock, Peter; Fenway; An Unexpurgated History of the Boston Red Sox (New York: G.P. Putnam's Sons,1992) 221.

22. Boston *Daily Record*, April 16, 1945.

23. Boston *Guardian*, April 14, 1945.

24. Golenbock, Peter; Fenway; An Unexpurgated History of the Boston Red Sox (New York: G.P. Putnam's Sons,1992) 222.

25. New York *Post* , April 17, 1959 (from the Schomburg clipping file: part I).

26. Boston *Globe*, April 29, 1959.

27. Golenbock, Peter; Fenway; An Unexpurgated History of the Boston Red Sox (New York: G.P. Putnam's Sons,1992) 222.

28. Interview with Joe Cashman from: Golenbock, Peter; Fenway; An Unexpurgated History of the Boston Red Sox (New York: G.P. Putnam's Sons,1992) 222.

29. Boston *Chronicle*, April 21, 1945.

30. Boston *Chronicle*, May 5, 1945.

31. Boston *Chronicle*, April 21, 1945.

32. Boston Guardian, April 21, 1945.

33. Interview with Doris Bunte

34. Interview with Doris Bunte

35. Patterson, James T. Grand Expectations: The United States 1945-1974 (New York: Oxford University Press, 1996) 316.

36. *The Sporting News*, March 18, 1959.

37. *The Sporting News*, March 18, 1959, April 18, 1959.

38. *The Sporting News*, March 18, 1959.

39. Interview with Doris Bunte.

40. Chicago *Defender*, January 31, 1959.

41. Chicago *Defender*, March 7, 1959.

42. *The Sporting News*, February 18, 1959.

43. Chicago *Defender*, March 7, 1959.

44. Boston *Daily Record*, March 7, 1959.

45. *The Sporting News*, April 1, 1959.

46. Interview with Pumpsie Green.

47. *The Sporting News*, March 4, 1959.

48. *The Sporting News*, March 18, 1959.

49. *Boston Daily Record*, July 31, 1959.

50. Boston *Chronicle*, March 14, 1959.

51. Boston *Chronicle*, March 14, 1959.

52. Boston *Daily Record*, March 7, 1959.

53. Boston *Daily Record*, March 7, 1959.

54. Boston *Daily Record*, April 8, 1959.

55. Interview with Pumpsie Green.

56. Boston *Herald*, April 8, 1959.

57. Michigan *Chronicle*, April 18, 1959.

58. Boston *Herald*, April 9, 1959.

59. Boston *Daily Record*, April 9, 1959.

60. Boston *Daily Record*, April 10, 1959.

61. Boston *Herald*, April 9,1959.

62. Boston *Daily Record*, April 11, 1959.

63. Boston Globe, April 8, 1959.

64. Boston globe, April 8, 1959.

65. Boston globe, April 8, 1959.

66. Boston globe, April 8, 1959.

67. Boston globe, April 8, 1959.

68. Boston globe, April 8, 1959.

69. Hirshberg, Al., <u>What's the Matter with the Red Sox</u> (New York: Dodd, Mead) 143.

70. Boston *Herald*, April 9, 1959.

71. Interview with Pumpsie Green.

72. Boston *Daily Record*, April 9, 1959.

73. Boston *Chronicle*, April 11, 1959.

74. Boston *Daily Record*, April 15, 1959.

75. Boston *Globe*, April 11, 1959.

76. Boston *Daily Record*, April 15, 1959.

77. Boston *Globe*, April 12, 1959.

78. Boston *Globe*, April 12, 1959.

79. Boston *Daily Record*, April 14, 1959.

80. Chicago *Defender*, May 2, 1959.

81. Boston Globe, April 22, 1959.

82. Chicago *Defender*, May 2, 1959.

83. Chicago *Defender*, May 2, 1959.

84. Boston *Chronicle*, April 18, 1959.

85. Interview with Doris Bunte

86. Boston *Daily Record*, June 4, 1959.

87. Boston *Daily Record*, July 22, 1959.

88. Boston *Evening Record*, July 22, 1959.

89. Boston *Globe*, July 24, 1959.

90. Boston *Herald*, July 23, 1959.

91. Boston *Chronicle*, July 25, 1959.

92. Boston *Chronicle*, May 2, 1959.

93. Boston *Globe*, April 8, 1959.

94. Chicago *Defender*, August 1, 1959.

Made in the USA
Monee, IL
02 August 2021

74777761R00032